THAT THEY ALL MAY BE ONE

*"That they all may be one,
as You, Father, are in Me, and I in You;
that they also may be one in Us,
that the world may believe
that You sent Me."*

John 17:21

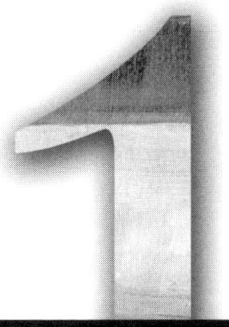

THAT THEY ALL MAY BE ONE

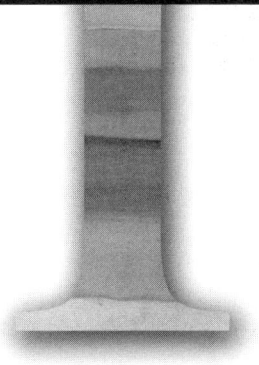

K.P. YOHANNAN

a division of Gospel for Asia

www.gfa.org

That They All May Be One
© 2003 by K.P. Yohannan
All rights reserved.
All Scripture quotations, unless otherwise indicated, are taken from the New King James Version. Copyright © 1982 by Thomas Nelson, Inc. Used by permission. All rights reserved. Scripture quotations marked NLT are taken from the Holy Bible, New Living Translation, copyright © 1996. Used by permission of Tyndale House Publishers, Inc., Wheaton, IL 60189, USA. All rights reserved.
Verses marked NIV are taken from the HOLY BIBLE, NEW INTERNATIONAL VERSION®. Copyright © 1973, 1978, 1984 Biblica. Used by permission of Zondervan. All rights reserved.
ISBN: 978-1-59589-011-5
Sixth printing, 2012
Published by gfa books, a division of Gospel for Asia
WWW.GFA.ORG

Table of Contents

Introduction	9
1. Fitted Together	11
2. Vital Differences	15
3. The Bond of Perfection	27
4. Choose the Low Road	35
5. Watch the Lamb	43
Concluding Remarks	49
Notes	51

Introduction

One of my all-time favorite books is *The Calvary Road* by Roy Hession. This book was written in the context of a group of missionaries working and experiencing a time of revival together. In the introduction of the book, Norman P. Grubb writes,

> We [the group of missionaries] are beginning to learn, as a company of Christ's witnesses, that the rivers of life to the world do not flow out in their fullness through one man, but through the body, the team. Our brokenness and openness must be two-way, horizontal as well as vertical, with one another as with God. We are just beginning to experience in our

own ranks that team work in the Spirit is one of the keys to revival, and that we have to learn and practice the laws of a living fellowship.[1]

It is my prayer that the Lord would give us an understanding of true unity and help us to put into practice the "laws of a living fellowship." We were not called to be individuals doing our own thing. We were called into the *family* of God, to oneness and unity with Him and with our fellowman.

May we strive to maintain this unity, each day linking arms with our brothers and sisters, genuinely loving each other and laboring together to see the kingdom of God come.

CHAPTER ONE

Fitted Together

———•••———

In 1 Kings 18:31, when the prophet Elijah repaired the broken altar, we are told he used 12 stones, "according to the number of the tribes of the sons of Jacob, to whom the word of the LORD had come . . ." This is an interesting statement, because at the time of this account the children of Israel were splintered into various groups, fragmented and backslidden in heart. Yet despite their condition, God still referred to them as one, together chosen as His children. It was on that restored altar, with the stones representing the 12 tribes of Israel, that God made His great power known by defeating the prophets of Baal.

But consider this: Would that altar have been complete with only 11 of the stones or

8 of the stones representing the tribes of Israel? No, it would not have been. It was *all* 12 stones that were recognized by God and *all* 12 through which He made His power known.

We can learn a lot from this Old Testament example. Another beautiful illustration of how we are to be united as one is found in the temple Solomon built in Jerusalem. It is said that each stone used in its building was chipped at and carved away until it fit perfectly with the stones around it—so perfectly that no mortar was even needed to hold them together. Each individual stone fit perfectly with the others, becoming *one* beautiful temple for the Lord. This is what the Lord desires for us today.

You see, rather than dwelling in a temple made with human hands as in the days of old, God has now chosen instead to dwell within you and me, His temple made with *living stones* (see 1 Peter 2:5). Like the stones used to build the temple, God desires His living stones to fit together perfectly by the unity of His Spirit and the bond of love.

The kingdom of God is a relational kingdom. Think about it; Jesus didn't ask us to pray only alone. He said, "For where *two or three* are gathered together in My name, I am there in the midst of them" (Matthew 18:20, emphasis mine). Neither did He send out the disciples individually but rather two by two (see Mark 6). His purpose in doing things this way was so that they would be able to minister to each other and support one another as they reached out to the lost around them, and so that the world, by observing the disciples' love for one another, would know the love of God.

During Jesus' last few moments before going to the cross, He left His disciples not with a series of steps on how to reach the lost. He did not sit them down with notebooks and pens or have them memorize certain methods, techniques or anything else. To prepare them for the enormous task ahead, He simply left this powerful statement: "By this all men will know that you are my disciples, if you *love one another*" (John 13:35, NIV, emphasis mine).

What is disunity except the lack of love? When we recognize the importance that Jesus placed upon loving one another above all else, and we begin to walk in obedience to His command, nothing will be able to hinder us from seeing the kingdom of God come in our generation!

CHAPTER TWO

Vital Differences

———•••———

Look at your body and you will see a left leg and a right leg, a nose and two eyes. We were all given two feet and two hands. Both hands are complete with five fingers—nothing is missing. And because nothing is missing, you are able to write with your hand and feed yourself as well. You can see with your eyes and walk with your feet, doing all the things your brain tells you to do.

Imagine now if some parts of your body were missing or were sick and not working. Have you ever seen someone try to walk without their big toe? We typically consider a missing leg or missing arm a big deal—and it is. Yet how many times have you considered the importance of your big toe? This one little body part may seem insignificant and not all that impressive or important, but it establishes the balance for the entire body, keeping you steady and able to walk. You wouldn't even be able to stand without it! How crucial this small, seemingly insignificant member really is.

Just like the toe or the leg, the arm or the nose, each one of us represents a different, unique and valuable part of the Body of Christ. Each part is needed so that the Body is complete, able to do whatever is required.

The Bible speaks of the importance of each member, big or small, known or unknown, honored or not, in 2 Corinthians. In writing to the believers there, Paul reminds them how each individual is vital and contributes to the health of the whole:

> Yes, the body has many different parts, not just one part. If the foot says, "I am not a part of the body because I am not a hand," that does not make it any less a part of the body. And if the ear says, "I am not part of the body because I am only an ear and not an eye," would that make it any less a part of the body? Suppose the whole body were an eye—then how would you hear? Or if your whole body were just one big ear, how could you smell anything?

Vital Differences

> But God made our bodies with many parts, and he has put each part just where he wants it. What a strange thing a body would be if it had only one part! Yes, there are many parts, but only one body. The eye can never say to the hand, "I don't need you." The head can't say to the feet, "I don't need you. . . . "
>
> This makes for harmony among the members, so that all the members care for each other equally. If one part suffers, all the parts suffer with it, and if one part is honored, all the parts are glad.
>
> Now all of you together are Christ's body, and each one of you is a separate and necessary part of it (1 Corinthians 12:14–21, 25–27, NLT).

Just as the Lord has caused everything in our physical bodies to function so perfectly, so He also has done with us, His spiritual Body. I have traveled to numerous places and have seen many different groups of believers. There are differences in each fellowship, and the meshing of these differences is what makes the Body of Christ so beautiful.

The first place that comes to mind is Gospel for Asia's international headquarters in the United States and the group of people the Lord has brought together to serve there. He brings the young and the old, the strong and the weak, the slow and the eager. There are people from different places, backgrounds and experiences, yet each one is greatly needed and fits together in the service of the Lord. No one is perfect alone, but each person's skills, abilities, talents, giftings and temperaments make the ministry whole and complete.

A Blessing in the Difference

In the illustration of the parts of the body all being important, unity seems to be an obvious element, easily attained. But as you and I both know, it's not always as easy as it sounds.

Differences are just that—they separate and distinguish one from another. And unless we put forth an effort to live in unity, our differences can be used to divide us, causing great chasms and hurts.

I have had many personal experiences with both knowing the pain and the beautiful purpose of differences. Back in the early days of the ministry, when Gospel for Asia (GFA) was just starting out, a brother named Fred came to work with us. I had the hardest time working with this man. He was just so different from me. We were complete opposites—I was night; he was day. His skin is clean white; mine is dark brown. That is what you'd see on the surface, but the differences ran much deeper than that. We had different personali-

Vital Differences

ties and different ways of doing things; we were different in every way you could possibly imagine. We just couldn't seem to get along. It was absolutely awful.

There were many times when I went through such agony working with Fred. Being the leader of GFA, I thought I could just ask him to leave. "I cannot live with him anymore. He just does not understand!" We obviously could not get along and because this was causing so much added tension to my days, I decided Fred must go.

The day before I was going to call it quits with him, God, in His mercy and grace, intervened. In the evening when I was all alone, God began to speak to me about the struggles I had with Fred. Surely He knew of my agony with this man and would agree with me about the pain this situation was causing me. Or so I thought. I didn't expect to hear God say, "The problem is not Fred. It's you." This shocked me! "What?" I said, "Me, the problem? God, You know how I've been living with all these issues with this man!" He said, "Yes, I know, but it's you that is the problem."

Later the next day, God continued to speak to me and said, "I have a plan and you never understood it. You only looked at the work. You only looked at what you could get out of Fred. You only looked at how fast he could run. You only looked at how well he spoke and what he did to see if it met your qualifications. You only looked at how he could perform from your perspective, with you as his judge. You never understood Me."

I broke down and cried. God was right. The problem *was* with me.

This incident was a major turning point in my life. I never did fire Fred; instead, I asked him to forgive me. Although Fred's temperament never changed and neither did mine, my heart changed inside that day.

I can honestly tell you, since that day I have never had anger, unforgiveness or an unloving heart toward my brother Fred. As a matter of fact, I cannot imagine life at GFA without him. One of my greatest joys is that Fred and I—two entirely different people—work in the same kingdom's work, fighting side by side, both taking orders from Him who is our head. He has faithfully labored right alongside me for 22 years now. This is the kind of perfect and beautiful work God does to unify His Body.

In hindsight, I see how wonderful this situation was. God puts us with other people to show us how we need them and they need us, and together we grow and mature and do the part God created each of us to do.

As long as we human beings live together

Vital Differences

on this earth, there will be differences. We come from so many different backgrounds—family backgrounds, Christian backgrounds, educational backgrounds and cultural backgrounds. We differ in age, race, income and marital status. We must not concentrate on the differences as "negatives" but rather see them as good, bringing balance and fullness to our lives and to the rest of the Body. Yet it is only as we look to Christ that we can have the perspective of seeing our differences as blessings.

Recognize the Value

The Body of Christ is complete only because of differences.

Think about that statement for a moment. Consider how many different people, ministries, churches and mission organizations there are. Each has been given a particular assignment from God and carries with it different strengths and weaknesses. Whether we realize it or not, we all need each other. We cannot stand alone.

GFA's approach to ministry focuses on preaching the Gospel first and foremost. But recently, a doctor who heads up a large medical mission organization came to visit GFA to talk to us about the importance of hospital ministry—how Jesus healed people, and

That They All May Be One

through that healing He brought them to eternal salvation.

For a long time I sat with this man and listened to what he was sharing. He had many good things to say. By the time the meeting drew to a close, I saw the enormous potential God has given their ministry. The opportunities are endless, especially in Asian nations where illness and disease are so widespread. They could minister in places like Orissa, where the medical needs were so overwhelming after the devastating cyclone hit in 1999. Millions of people would turn to Christ through the compassion shown them in treating their sicknesses and in healing their diseases.

When he had finished talking, I said, "You are absolutely right. What you are saying works beautifully if the preaching of the Gospel is not compromised."

Ten years ago, I never would have responded so well; in fact, I would not have even considered this kind of ministry. If someone had come and talked to me like that doctor did, I would have said, "Yeah, okay. That is all very nice, but I will see you later. Here at GFA we preach the Gospel. I don't have room for anything that is less important."

Of course preaching the Gospel must always be the priority. But at the same time,

Jesus still fed the hungry and healed the sick. If we, Christ's Body, are to function like He did, we have to accept the value of each and every individual part. If GFA didn't accept the ministry of this medical mission, valuing the role it plays, then the work of both groups would be compromised.

Wherever you are and with whomever the Lord has joined you together, remember that you and your brother or sister have each been given a particular part to play. As we recognize our part, our gifts and our lack, we can complement each others' lives and experience the harmony of the fullness of Christ. Every individual that the Lord has brought into your life, especially in the service of the Lord, is uniquely placed to somehow complement your lack in the Body and you, theirs. In accepting and valuing each person and who they are, the whole Body functions smoothly.

Unseen Yet Needed

Just as there are different organs in your human body that you have never seen yet are vital to your existence, so there are members in the Body of Christ. Perhaps you or someone around you is rarely noticed, always working behind the scenes, not given much honor or fame. Remember that "the last will be first, and the first last" (Matthew 20:16).

And "he who is greatest among you shall be your servant" (Matthew 23:11).

Although you can't see your heart, your kidneys or your stomach, if one of these hidden members stops functioning properly, you would certainly know. You would be very sick and possibly in the hospital.

The same is true concerning the Body of Christ. The healthy functioning of every part is critical. When each member is healthy and rightly connected to the rest of the Body, all is well. But when one member of the Body is no longer connected to the whole, that member is in danger of dying. And it is not just that part that suffers, but the whole Body is also affected.

United like this, we realize we are linked to each other, walking side by side, feeling each other's victories as well as each other's hurts. It is like when I stub my toe—ouch!—my whole body feels it! I hop around on the other foot and hold my toe with my hand. Maybe a little tear runs down my cheek because it hurts so badly. Galatians 6:2 says, "Bear one another's burdens, and so fulfill the law of Christ." Romans 12:15–16 (NIV) says, "Rejoice with those who rejoice; mourn with those who mourn. Live in harmony with one another." That means if my brother is sad, I am sad too. If my sister is sick, I feel her sickness.

Vital Differences

In 1994 a terrible butchering happened in the African nation of Rwanda. In the span of just a few months, more than 700,000 people were killed in a conflict between neighboring tribes, the Hutus and the Tutsis. After hearing reports of this tragedy, can you remember what happened in your church service the following Sunday? In the church I attended, absolutely nothing was different. Everything continued as normal, as if this slaughtering of thousands never even happened. There were no tears, no hurt, no pain, no sharing—nothing.

This concerns me. Much of Christendom has come to focus its effort on sustaining its own emotional health, strength and comfort. Lukewarm Christianity watches those who share in the pain of the suffering and says, "That is fanaticism! That is flesh! It's all emotion!" Lukewarm Christianity won't let its heart be broken for the hurt and dying. But biblical Christianity sees the tragedy and is moved by the pain and suffering, weeping just as Jesus wept over Jerusalem (see Luke 19:41).

In the parable of the Good Samaritan, the proper religious people left the wounded man to die on the road. Only the man from Samaria had compassion and shared the pain, helping his brother who was in need (see Luke 10).

We cannot generate Christlike compassion or godly emotions any more than we can save ourselves. But we can be obedient to pray for and receive His burden, even if it means processing painful things. I am not saying this to make you feel like you're not praying enough or not doing enough or not feeling enough of the burden. All I want is for us to take His yoke and share with Him in "the fellowship of His sufferings" (see Philippians 3:10).

And just as we share in the sufferings, we also share in the victories and joys. If there is rejoicing in heaven when one sinner repents, then there should be rejoicing on earth too! In Luke 10, we find the story of Jesus sending out the disciples two by two to heal the sick. Luke 10:17 says, "Then the seventy returned with joy, saying, 'Lord, even the demons are subject to us in Your name.' " Seeing how excited His disciples were at the power of God, Jesus *rejoiced with them*. Luke 10:21 says, "In that hour Jesus rejoiced in the Spirit and said, 'I thank You, Father, Lord of heaven and earth, that You have hidden these things from the wise and prudent and revealed them to babes.' "

Let us then imitate Jesus, rejoice in our differences and make the effort to see the value and gifts each of us brings to the whole. In this appreciation of each other and how the Lord has made us, He will be glorified.

CHAPTER THREE

The Bond of Perfection

Have you ever seen a boxing match between a left arm and a right arm of the same person? Does your little finger purposely scratch and hurt your ring finger? If you are cold, does one of your feet try to block out the other foot to get closer to the heater? No, of course not. To even speak of such things seems absolutely ridiculous. But, I tell you, this sort of ridiculous fighting goes on in the Body of Christ all too often.

One of the things I fear most in ministry of any kind is the disunity that the devil is able to create. When disunity prevails, the work of the Lord is destroyed. Satan knows very well that "any kingdom divided against itself will be ruined, and a house divided against itself will fall" (Luke 11:17, NIV). And seeing how Satan cringes at the thought of the kingdom of God advancing, he does not want the house of the Lord to stand. So he takes the very differences that were meant to complete us and uses them to divide us. Whether it is differences in theology and doctrine or styles of worship and prayer—any difference you can imagine—Satan will use them to sow seeds of strife and disunity.

This is the reason why God so justly and immediately dealt with anything that hindered the unity of the children of Israel throughout the Old Testament. Whenever God asked His people to go forward, He would first weed out whatever held them back from moving ahead united in heart and mind. In Numbers 16, we read the story of Korah, the man whom the ground opened up and swallowed after he refused to acknowledge Moses as God's appointed leader. In Numbers 12, God punished the fractionating spirit of Miriam and Aaron. When the 12 spies came back with divided reports about the prospects of taking over the Promised Land, God punished the dissenting 10 spies who had not trusted Him (see Numbers 14).

The Bond of Perfection

What *(or Who)* is the Problem?

When I was 18, I traveled throughout India as part of an Operation Mobilization evangelistic team. We would share the Gospel with people in different towns and villages, selling tracts and other Christian literature at a very low price. With the money we made selling the literature, we bought food to eat and keep us alive.

Our team was made up of all Indian brothers except for our team leader, Brother William. He was a tall Englishman, 6 foot 2 inches or so, who previously studied as a medical student but walked away from it all so that he could reach the lost in Asia. He was always a very nice and gentle man. As our team leader, Brother William was responsible for making decisions in the group. I served alongside him as the assistant team leader, and was expected to take care of the problems of the Indians on the team.

After working with Brother William for a couple of weeks, it was obvious to me that everything he did was simply done in the wrong way. He didn't understand the culture or do things the Indian way. It got so bad that I was afraid the team wouldn't survive with him in charge. He was never very concerned about washing his clothes or keeping clean. When he would get ready for bed at night, his trousers were so stiff with dirt and grime that they almost stood up on their own. And he smelled too. On top of all that, we could never sell enough books, and so we were half-starving. He would take us from one street vendor to the next, asking, "Chapati, how much it cost?" (Chapati is similar to a tortilla.) Then he would ask, "Dal free?" (Dal is like a lentil soup.) In some places, if you buy enough chapatis, the dal is free. Wherever the dal was free, we would buy the chapati and eat. But not very many places gave free dal. So in the horrible heat we would follow this white man, going from one vendor to the next, trying to find a place to eat for as little money as possible. We were half-starving, dirty, sick and selling very few books.

I must honestly confess, although Brother William was from England and was older than I was, I knew I could manage the team better than he. Many of the decisions he made seemed totally off the wall. Our ministry was ineffective. There was no unity on the team at all. Nothing was working.

One day I just couldn't take it anymore. When the team gathered for our prayer meeting in the morning, I declared a boycott. I said, "Brother William, you cannot be the leader! You just are not able. You are an English man. You don't understand Indian ways.

The Bond of Perfection

You take us like beggars looking for food. You stink. The literature is not being sold. You are not a good example for us, and you don't care about us. Whoever made you our leader made a big mistake. We cannot cooperate with you anymore." Everyone was on my side.

I still remember that day. I can see Brother William's face so clearly. He didn't say one word. He simply sat there and cried. That's all he did. Tears poured down his face, and all of us Indians on the team, including me, sat there and didn't know what to do. All of a sudden, it was like the Lord walked right into my heart and convicted me, "You are sinning against Me. You are rebelling."

I broke down weeping, realizing the magnitude of what I had just done. I cried, "Brother William, please forgive me. Look, I touch your feet. I will be your servant. Even if you starve me to death, even if you want me to work all day and all night long, I will obey you as long as you are my leader. I will never fight with you or against you again." I turned to my Indian brothers as well and said, "I have done wrong. Please forgive me."

That day I saw the hand of God holding Brother William. I saw the man's weaknesses and his struggles. When he first came to India, he was tall and well-built, with his muscles bulging out. In a few months' time, he was all skin and bones because he lived just like us. He lived on the streets, ate simple food, suffered from diarrhea and had all the other problems we had. For the first time I saw Brother William's sacrifice. And I saw God using him to take me from where I was to a much higher place—to a place of humility and genuine love for my brother.

After this incident, things went along so smoothly. Our team life was wonderful. I loved Brother William like my own life. I have wonderful memories of those times. He never changed. He didn't start washing his trousers or getting us more food. But I changed. We never had disunity or problems after that because God had dealt with the problem—with me. I, the one who "knew" how things should run, had been the cause of the disunity all along.

Put on Love

"Therefore, as the elect of God, holy and beloved, put on tender mercies, kindness, humility, meekness, longsuffering; bearing with one another, and forgiving one another, if anyone has a complaint against another; even as Christ forgave you, so you also must do. But above all these things put on love, which is the bond of perfection" (Colossians 3:12–14).

The Bond of Perfection

"Love suffers long and is kind; love does not envy; love does not parade itself, is not puffed up; does not behave rudely, does not seek its own, is not provoked, thinks no evil; does not rejoice in iniquity, but rejoices in the truth; bears all things, believes all things, hopes all things, endures all things. Love never fails" (1 Corinthians 13:4–8).

All disunity begins with a lack of genuine, godly love for one another. That's where it all starts. When Satan gets in and stirs up strife and hurt, love dries up and things go downhill from there. This is also when the work we are doing for God comes to a standstill. As long as disunity abounds, all ministry will be tainted and ineffective. But when our hearts are cleansed and changed, softened and broken, ministry becomes a simple overflow of a heart filled with love from Christ for all men.

CHAPTER FOUR

Choose the Low Road

———•••———

> Therefore if there is any consolation in Christ, if any comfort of love, if any fellowship of the Spirit, if any affection and mercy, fulfill my joy by being like-minded, having the same love, being of one accord, of one mind. Let nothing be done through selfish ambition or conceit, but in lowliness of mind. Let each esteem others better than himself. Let each of you look out not only for his own interests, but also for the interests of others (Philippians 2:1–4).

The essence of this Scripture is that unity and humility work hand in hand. Unity comes from love, love comes from humility, and humility comes by submitting to one another. When there is no humility, there is no unity. Mother Teresa once said, "Humility is the mother of all virtues. It is in being humble that our love becomes real, devoted and ardent. If you are humble nothing will touch you, neither praise nor disgrace, because you know what you are."[1] She also said, "To love and to be loved, we must know our brothers and sisters. For knowledge always leads to love and love in action is service. Our work is only the expression of the love we have for God."[2] Romans 12:10 pleads with us to "be kindly affectionate to one another with brotherly love, in honor giving preference to one another."

I used to be a fighter. I fought for my doctrines. I fought for my way of ministry. I must have been one of the most difficult human beings to live or work with. I won every argument and always got things to go the way I wanted them to. But in reality, every argument I won I really lost because I lost the people—I alienated the Body of Christ around me. Every time I won, I hurt my brothers and sisters, as well as God, because I would not choose to do things His way—the way of love and humility. But praise God that He didn't give up on me. Slowly I began to understand the importance of submitting to my brothers and to my sisters, truly loving them.

Willing to Bend

I used to be absolutely radical about my theological doctrines. Even now, there is a whole theological world that fights over so many different points of view on a variety of subjects. Volumes are written containing thousands of pages debating these different opinions. Yet the root of all these arguments and debates is really hardness of heart and a lack of love. Any doctrine or form of "Christianity" that is not spoken and upheld in love, that induces people to continually fight for their side, creates disunity and rips the Body of Christ apart.

When we handle our pain, our rights, our gifts or our talents without love, we are walking on dangerous ground. It does not matter how right we may be in standing for truth—if what we say is not done in the love and humility of Christ, disunity will result. But there is joy and life in giving in to the ways of God and being broken and humbled.

A few years ago I attended a pastors conference in California. I was scheduled to share on missions along with a couple other speakers from across the United States. To be honest, I didn't like one of the other plenary speakers at this missions conference. This man had written some articles that I thought were really destructive to the work of God.

That They All May Be One

As I remembered the things he wrote, I began to get very upset over the whole situation. I couldn't believe he was invited to the conference to speak on missions. As I started to speak before the assembly full of people, I made an unkind, unloving comment about him. I considered myself justified in what I said because I thought the damage he did to the kingdom's work was great.

Directly from this missions conference, I flew to India. While I was there, the Lord began to speak to my heart and show me how I had spoken wrongly. As soon as I came back to the GFA office in the United States, I knew what I needed to do. I had to call and ask forgiveness from the man who invited me to speak at that conference. But what I said was not just a private thing—it was public, involving many people. So when I called him, I said, "Would you please do me a favor? Next time you write to all of the pastors who attended that conference, would you please tell them I ask their forgiveness for having made that statement? It was not in the Spirit of love or the Spirit of Christ that I spoke it, and I am sorry."

Do you think this was easy for me to do? Not at all! Each one of us has our pride, our knowledge and our own way we think is right. But what we know will never justify us saying anything rude or unkind. Remember the

Choose the Low Road

famous chapter in 1 Corinthians that says,

> Though I speak with the tongues of men and of angels, but have not love, I have become sounding brass or a clanging cymbal. And though I have the gift of prophecy, and understand all mysteries and all knowledge, and though I have all faith, so that I could remove mountains, but have not love, I am nothing. And though I bestow all my goods to feed the poor, and though I give my body to be burned, but have not love, it profits me nothing (1 Corinthians 13:1–3).

The beauty of this whole incident is that when I humbled myself and sought forgiveness, this man that I had spoken against responded back to me. He had received the letter that was sent to all who attended the conference and read of my asking forgiveness. He called me and thanked me for my humility, saying, "Brother K.P., no wonder God is using you so much. No wonder God's grace is upon your life." And I said, "Thank you for saying that to me." God knows how hard it was for me to humble myself and ask for forgiveness. But He is faithful to give us the grace and strength to submit to others and admit when we are wrong.

But this doesn't mean we must always say, "Yes, yes" to everything. Maybe we know that someone's actions or beliefs are wrong or the way we've been treated is not right. We don't just pretend these things are okay for the sake of keeping the peace. Instead, what we need to do is commit these situations to God and let it go into His hands, praying for our brother or sister, asking God to give us wisdom and to work things out His way. William Barclay once said, "In our dealings with men, however unkind and hurting they are, we must exercise the same patience as God exercises with us. It is simple truth that such patience is not the sign of weakness but the sign of strength; it is not defeatism, but rather the only way to victory."[3]

In 1 Corinthians 5, Paul describes a situation of a man living in blatant, unconfessed sin. It took great love for Paul to put this man out of the church. Maybe it sounds horrible and unkind, but Paul did it with a firm, tough love. And look at the result. In 2 Corinthians 2, that man was restored to fellowship again. This kind of love—God's kind of love—always brings unity to the Body of Christ. It is a tough yet humble love that gives in but doesn't give up.

Unity in Action

If we really desire to be like Jesus and to walk in love and power as He did, we must

Choose the Low Road

humble ourselves.

We cannot just underline Scriptures on humility in our Bibles and never implement them into our lives. Scripture is practical, and we must live it out to experience its transforming power in our lives and relationships. We have to be willing to bend and break, to live a life not thinking of ourselves more highly than we ought to think. We have to honor and give preference to one another in real ways, everyday (see Romans 12:3, 10).

Because Scripture tells us to humble ourselves (see James 4:10), let us look for ways to do just that. Let us seize the opportunities God puts before us to love our neighbors as ourselves and to consider them better than ourselves. Be sensitive to other's needs, and when you are wrong, say so. "I am sorry for saying that. I didn't know it would hurt you. I didn't mean it that way." Often I am not sensitive enough to even know when I am being insensitive! Let us all pray, "Lord, make me more sensitive to my brothers and sisters."

This is what I believe the Lord desires for each and every person who confesses His name, whether in full-time ministry or not. God is looking for lowly hearts that are ready to be filled with His love and power. He is looking for a Body ready to be broken for the millions who are spiritually starving because they do not know Jesus. Only to the measure in which we are willing to bend and submit to one another will we experience Christ's unity and love that can bind us together. And it is the people who dwell in unity who will receive His blessing (see Psalm 133).

CHAPTER FIVE

Watch the Lamb

———•••———

Philippians 2:5–9 says, "Let this mind be in you which was also in Christ Jesus, who, being in the form of God, did not consider it robbery to be equal with God, but made Himself of no reputation, taking the form of a bondservant, and coming in the likeness of men. And being found in appearance as a man, He humbled Himself and became obedient to the point of death, even the death of the cross. Therefore God also has highly exalted Him and given Him the name which is above every name."

When Jesus humbled Himself in the last unequaled step of humility and love by dying on the cross, Scripture says that, "Therefore, God also has highly exalted Him." Love and humility is the road that leads us to unity and oneness, and it is the same road Christ walked while on this earth. When we see Him and the extent of His love and humility, choosing the low road, we begin to understand the power of humbling ourselves before our brothers and sisters, just as Jesus did. Consider the words written by the prophet Isaiah about our Lord, the Lamb of God:

> He was *despised and rejected by men*, a man of sorrows, and familiar with suffering. Like one from whom men hide their faces he was despised, and *we esteemed him not*. We all, like sheep, have gone astray, each of us has turned to *his own way*; and the LORD has laid on him the iniquity of us all. *He was oppressed and afflicted, yet he did not open his mouth; he was led like a lamb to the slaughter, and as a sheep before her shearers is silent, so he did not open his mouth* (Isaiah 53:3, 6–7, NIV, emphasis mine).

Think about the magnitude of these verses. The Son of God, who was there when the heavens and earth were first formed, chose to come to this earth not as an esteemed and highly respected man, but as a helpless baby born in a dirty stable to a poor, unwed mother. To take it further, He died the death of a lawbreaker. The only perfect man ever to live without sin on this earth died on a cross between two thieves. Even with 12 legions of angels at His disposal (see Matthew 26:53) ready and able to stop this great injustice from happening, Jesus chose to remain there—to be broken and humbled and to die. If ever there were a man with the right to fight for himself and against the wrong done to him, it would have been Jesus. But He did not. He never opened His mouth against His accusers or in His own defense, but only said, "Father, forgive them . . . " (Luke 23:34).

Only when I compare myself with Christ am I able to humble myself with all of my heart. What breaks relationships and sows disunity is my thinking I am better than somebody else, that my way is right or that my conviction is better than another's. But when I compare myself with Christ, who am I? Who am I to say, "I am right"? Who am I to stand up for the way I think things should be? Scripture says, "Let this mind be in you which was also in Christ Jesus, who, being in the form of God, did not consider it robbery to be equal with God, but made Himself of no reputation, taking the form of a bondservant" (Philippians 2:5–7).

It is when we choose to have "this mind in us," to see Jesus and follow Him in our relationships, that He will be exalted in our

That They All May Be One

lives, in our brother's life, in the Church and throughout the nations. Is this not our ultimate goal, to exalt and bring honor to the name of Christ? When we choose to walk in love and humility toward one another as He did—even to the very ones who crucified Him—we will see Him exalted. The world will know we are His disciples by our love for each other, and they will come to bow before Him because of this love.

Recently a brother who serves with our movement came to me upset about a particular situation involving some of the people he works with. When he came to talk to me about it, I knew from the moment he entered the room how upset he was.

"Please! I did not come to argue with you, Brother K.P.," he said. "You are my leader. I will do anything you tell me to do. Just let me tell you the facts." And so—one, two, three, four, five—he laid out for me the whole story, explaining all that had happened and how he was right. Then he raised his voice a little, and I could hear the pain in it as he said, "Brother K.P., tell me, am I wrong?"

I had to calm down because I didn't want to raise my voice as well. I said, "You know, you are absolutely right." I think he was expecting that I would argue with him or point out something wrong. But I said, "You are perfectly right." And he was. But my question to him was this: "Was *your* attitude in the situation Christlike? Was *your* response Christlike? Did they hear the mercy and love of Jesus in *your* voice? Did they see *in you* His grace and forgiveness?"

There was silence, and then the conversation continued. I said, "Even though you are correct, would you still ask others to forgive you for your lack of love in handling the situation? Would you bend and break even when you are right?" Jesus did. He could have come down from the cross and proven He was God. But Jesus didn't do it this way. And by the grace of God, neither did this brother. The next day, even though he was right and the facts were in his favor, he went and asked the others involved in the situation to forgive him.

It is this kind of submission and humility that binds us together and through which Christ is exalted in our lives and on the earth. What I am finding out about myself in dealing with people is that the problem is not outside. It is not the people who keep coming to me, pestering me, beating me, calling me names and telling me how to do things. The problem is that my own heart doesn't want to bend and break and respond as Christ would, in genuine love and humility.

Let us strive toward this end. "Therefore be

imitators of God as dear children. And walk in love, as Christ also has loved us and given Himself for us, an offering and a sacrifice to God for a sweet-smelling aroma" (Ephesians 5:1–2).

Concluding Remarks

———•••———

Please let us not get stuck on the problems, doctrines, or differences that are bound to occur in living and serving with people. Instead, choose to get stuck on love, extending grace and compassion to your brother or sister, praying for them and loving them with the love of Christ. Remember Matthew 25:40: "Assuredly, I say to you, inasmuch as you did it to one of the least of these My brethren, you did it to Me."

You are part of the family of God—not fragmented, not divided—but with one heart, one soul and one mind. You are called to live together, strive together, pray together, suffer together, agonize together—and if need be die together—with your brothers and sisters for

That They All May Be One

the sake of a world that has never heard the name of the Lord Jesus. This is our privilege and this is our calling.

Let us all then love and live in unity as one Body, one in Him.

Prayer

We pray, O Lord, that You would continue to bind us together with love—love that covers a multitude of sins, love that is so patient, gentle, forgiving and caring. Love that does not go around finding people's faults and criticizing others but love that always gives in. Help us to be humble and broken and to consider others as better than ourselves. Make us more like You, Jesus.

If this booklet has been a blessing to you, I would really like to hear from you. You may write to Gospel for Asia, 1800 Golden Trail Court, Carrollton, TX 75010. Or send an email to kp@gfa.org.

Notes

Introduction

[1] Roy Hession, *The Calvary Road* (London: Christian Literature Crusade, 1950), pp. 8–9.

Chapter 4

[1] Mother Teresa of Calcutta, *The Joy in Loving: A Guide to Daily Living*, comp. Jaya Chalika and Edward Le Joly (New York, NY: Penguin Group USA, Inc., 2000), p. 363.

[2] *Ibid*, p. 359.

[3] Vernon McLellan, *20th Century Thoughts That Shaped the Church* (Wheaton, IL: Tyndale House Publishers, Inc., 2000), p. 208.

No Longer a Slumdog

Read about an abandoned girl who found hope at the end of the railroad tracks, a young boy who escaped after years of forced servitude, and many others whose lives have also been redeemed. You'll be captivated by this powerful move of God as K.P. Yohannan leads you on a journey through the slums and villages of South Asia into the hearts and lives of these precious children. (176 pages)

REVOLUTION
in World Missions

Step into the story of missionary statesman K.P. Yohannan and experience the world through his eyes. You will hang on every word—from the villages of India to the shores of Europe and North America. Watch out: His passion is contagious! (240 pages)

Order these or other titles online at GFA.ORG/ALLONE
Gospel for Asia, 1800 Golden Trail Court, Carrollton, TX 75010
Toll free: 1-800-WIN-Asia

Booklets by K.P. Yohannan

A Life of Balance
Remember learning how to ride a bike? It was all a matter of balance. The same is true for our lives. Learn how to develop that balance, which will keep your life and ministry healthy and honoring God. (80 pages)

Crisis in Leadership
Leadership is not all daisies. There are struggles and challenges that we hardly know exist until we are put into a position of authority. Join K.P. Yohannan as he addresses how to avoid the crises of leadership and press on to know Christ. (72 pages)

Dependence upon the Lord
Don't build in vain. Learn how to daily depend upon the Lord—whether in the impossible or the possible—and see your life bear lasting fruit. (48 pages)

Discouragement: Reasons and Answers
Ready to defeat discouragement and move on? It can be done! Discover the reasons for discouragement, and find hope and strength for an overcoming life. (56 pages)

Journey with Jesus
Take this invitation to walk the roads of life intimately with the Lord Jesus. Stand with the disciples and learn from Jesus' example of love, humility, power and surrender. (56 pages)

Learning to Pray
Whether you realize it or not, your prayers change things. Be hindered no longer as K.P. Yohannan shares how you can grow in your daily prayer life. See for yourself how God still does the impossible through prayer. (64 pages)

Living by Faith, Not by Sight
The promises of God are still true today: *"Anything is possible to him who believes!"* This balanced teaching will remind you of the power of God and encourage you to step out in childlike faith. (56 pages)

Principles in Maintaining a Godly Organization
Remember the "good old days" in your ministry? This booklet provides a biblical basis for maintaining that vibrancy and commitment that accompany any new move of God. (48 pages)

Seeing Him
Do you often live just day-to-day, going through the routine of life? We so easily lose sight of Him who is our everything. Through this booklet, let the Lord Jesus restore your heart and eyes to see Him again. (48 pages)

Stay Encouraged
How are you doing? Discouragement can sneak in quickly and subtly, through even the smallest things. Learn how to stay encouraged in every season of life, no matter what the circumstances may be. (56 pages)

That They All May Be One
In this booklet, K.P. Yohannan opens up his heart and shares from past struggles and real-life examples on how to maintain unity with those in our lives. A must read! (56 pages)

The Beauty of Christ through Brokenness
We were made in the image of Christ that we may reflect all that He is to the hurting world around us. Rise above the things that hinder you from doing this, and see how your life can display His beauty, power and love. (72 pages)

The Lord's Work Done in the Lord's Way
Tired? Burned out? Weary? The Lord's work done in His way will never destroy you. Learn what it means to minister unto Him and keep the holy love for Him burning strong even in the midst of intense ministry. A must-read for every believer! (72 pages)

The Way of True Blessing
What does God value most? Find out in this booklet as K.P. Yohannan reveals truths from the life of Abraham, an ordinary man who became the friend of God. (56 pages)

When We Have Failed—What Next?
The best *is* yet to come. Do you find that hard to believe? If failure has clouded your vision to see God's redemptive power, this booklet is for you. God's ability to work out His best plan for your life remains. Believe it. (88 pages)

Order booklets online at GFA.ORG/ALLONE
Gospel for Asia, 1800 Golden Trail Court, Carrollton, TX 75010
Toll free: 1-800-WIN-ASIA

Travel to the mission field—for a few hours

Even though you don't live with the millions of people in South Asia or experience their unique cultures and struggles, you can intercede for them!

By joining in **Gospel for Asia's live-streaming prayer meetings**, you can step inside their world through stories, photos and videos. You might even change, too. Here's what other people said about the prayer meetings:

"I don't think I ever come away with a dry eye from these prayer meetings. It is so encouraging to me to see the Lord working so mightily in so many ways in the world."
—Sheri

"It is so good and helpful to hear of the needs and to sense God's Spirit at work. It helps me to pray more earnestly and to be a part of what God is doing in your ministry."
—Timothy

"Praise Jesus! I love having a team to pray with." —Mia

Pray with us!
Go to **gfa.org/pray** for schedules and to participate in the streamed prayer meetings.